W9-CLF-135

Body Fuel for Healthy Bodies
Meat, Fish, Eggs, Nuts, and Beans

Trisha Sertori

Marshall Cavendish
Benchmark

New York

This edition first published in 2009 in the United States of America by Marshall Cavendish Benchmark.

Marshall Cavendish Benchmark
99 White Plains Road
Tarrytown, NY 10591
www.marshallcavendish.us

All Internet sites were available and accurate when sent to press.

First published in 2008 by
MACMILLAN EDUCATION AUSTRALIA PTY LTD
15–19 Claremont Street, South Yarra 3141

Visit our website at www.macmillan.com.au or go directly to www.macmillanlibrary.com.au

Associated companies and representatives throughout the world.

Copyright © Macmillan Education Australia 2008

Library of Congress Cataloging-in-Publication Data

Sertori, Trisha.
   Meat, fish, eggs, nuts, and beans / by Trisha Sertori.
      p. cm. — (Body fuel for healthy bodies)
   Includes index.
   Summary: "Discusses the importance of a healthy, well-balanced diet,
   focusing on meats, fish, eggs, nuts, and beans"—Provided by publisher.
   ISBN 978-0-7614-3801-4
   1. Nutrition—Juvenile literature. 2. Food of animal origin—Juvenile literature.
   3. Nuts—Juvenile literature. 4. Beans—Juvenile literature. I. Title.
   TX355.S426 2009
   613.2—dc22

                2008026203

Edited by Margaret Maher
Text and cover design by Stella Vassiliou
Page layout by Stella Vassiliou
Photo research by Claire Francis
Illustrations by Toby Quarmby, Vishus Productions, pp. 4, 5; Jeff Lang and
  Stella Vassiliou, pp. 8, 9 (below), 10; all others by Stella Vassiliou.

Printed in the United States

Acknowledgments
The author and publishers are grateful to the following for permission to reproduce copyright material:

Cover and header photos courtesy of © iStockphoto.com (chop); © iStockphoto.com/Galina Barskaya (girl); © iStockphoto.com/Heather Down (beans); © iStockphoto.com/Inna Felker (leg of ham); © iStockphoto.com/George Peters (fish); © iStockphoto.com/Kristian Sekulic (boy); © iStockphoto.com/Marcelo Wain (nuts); Stella Vassiliou (eggs).

Photos courtesy of:
AAP Image/Wildlight, **23** (top); Artville/Burke Triolo Productions, **16** (bottom); Brand X Pictures, **30**; © Joe Gough/Dreamstime.com, **29** (middle); © Emin Ozkan/Dreamstime.com, **29** (2nd top); © Mosista Pambudi/Dreamstime.com, **7** (eggs); Getty Images/Dorling Kindersley, **12**; Getty Images/Ian O'Leary, **7** (tofu); Getty Images/Rayes, **15** (top); © onthehouse/Fotalia.com, **26**; © iStockphoto.com, **6** (sardine), **8**, **9** (middle, **10** (top), **19** (bottom), **22** (bottom left); © iStockphoto.com/John Bloor, **6** (top); © iStockphoto.com/Sandra Caldwell, **28** (top); © iStockphoto.com/Hugo Chang, **6** (oysters); © iStockphoto.com/Kelly Cline, **16** (middle), **20** (top); © iStockphoto.com/Andriy Doriy, **28** (3rd top); © iStockphoto.com/Peter Elvidge, **24**; © iStockphoto.com/Danny Hooks, **17** (bottom); © iStockphoto.com/Ashwin Kharidehal, **7** (nuts); © iStockphoto.com/David Lewis, **21**; © iStockphoto.com/Olga Lyubkina, **29** (top); © iStockphoto.com/Sandra O'Claire, **11** (top); © iStockphoto.com/Diane Rutt, **6** (prawns); © iStockphoto.com/Kevin Snair, **22** (bottom right); © iStockphoto.com/Leah-Anne Thompson, **18** (right); © iStockphoto.com/Guillermo Trejos, **14** (left); © iStockphoto.com/Sawayasu Tsuji, **28** (3rd bottom); MEA Photos/Lesya Bryndzia, **29** (bottom); Photolibrary/John Bavosi/Science Photo Library, **13** (left); Photolibrary/BSIP, **25** (right); Photolibrary/Loetscher Chlaus/Alamy, **22** (top left); Photolibrary/Martyn Evans/Alamy, **23** (middle); Photolibrary/F1 online/Alamy, **27** (left) Photolibrary/Tim Hill/Alamy, **16** (top); Photolibrary/Ladi Kirn/Alamy, **23** (bottom); Photolibrary/Paul Rapson /Science Photo Library, **19** (middle); Trisha Sertori, **18** (left); © Norman Chan/Shutterstock, **7** (soy beans), **28** (2nd bottom); © Ioannis Ioannou/Shutterstock, **28** (bottom); © Arnaud Weisser/Shutterstock, **28** (2nd top); © Lim Yong Hian/Shutterstock, **29** (2nd bottom); Stella Vassiliou, **1**, **3**; Ra Boe/Wikipedia, **22** (middle left).

MyPyramid symbols courtesy of U.S. Department of Agriculture.

While every care has been taken to trace and acknowledge copyright, the publisher tenders their apologies for any accidental infringement where copyright has proved untraceable. Where the attempt has been unsuccessful, the publisher welcomes information that would redress the situation.

1 3 5 6 4 2

Contents

Glossary Words

When a word is printed in **bold**, you can look up its meaning in the Glossary on page 31.

What Is Body Fuel?

Body fuel is the energy, vitamins, and minerals we need to live. Just as cars need gasoline and computers need electricity, people need energy, vitamins, and minerals to work.

The best way to fuel our bodies is with a **balanced diet**. A balanced diet gives us all the **nutrients** our bodies need.

Nutrients in Foods

The nutrients in foods are divided into macronutrients and micronutrients.

Macronutrients provide energy. They are proteins, carbohydrates, and fats and oils. Micronutrients help **chemical reactions** take place in the body. They are vitamins and minerals.

The Food Pyramid

The food pyramid lists foods for healthy bodies. The colors shown (from left to right) are for grains, vegetables, fruit, oils, dairy, and meat and beans.

MyPyramid.gov
STEPS TO A HEALTHIER YOU

Meat, Fish, Eggs, Nuts, and Beans

Meat, fish, eggs, nuts, and beans are high-protein foods. This food group fuels our body with the proteins we need to grow. Protein helps our bodies make amino acids, which build body tissues. Meat, fish, eggs, nuts, and beans are also rich in vitamins, minerals, and essential fatty acids.

The Food Pyramid

Meat, fish, eggs, nuts, and beans are found in the purple part of the food pyramid. Meat, fish, and eggs can be high in fat as well as protein. They should be eaten in moderation. Nuts and beans are rich in fiber, as well as proteins, and contain healthy fats.

People need different types of protein foods for a range of vitamins, minerals, and amino acids. Amino acids help us to grow, think, play, and even sleep.

Meat & Bean Group
Go lean with protein

MyPyramid.gov

What Types of Meat, Fish, Eggs, Nuts, and Beans Are There?

There are different types of meat, fish, eggs, nuts, and beans. They are all protein-rich foods. Some of these foods come from animals and some come from plants.

Meat
People around the world use meat as a protein source. Some Indigenous Australians hunt lizards and kangaroos. People in parts of Asia hunt deer, frogs, and insects, such as dragonflies, for protein. However, most people eat farmed beef, lamb, goat, poultry, or pork for protein.

Fish and Seafood
All fish and seafood supply protein. Some fish that are commonly eaten are flounder, tuna, and salmon. Animals that live in the sea but are not fish are called seafood. This includes shrimp, oysters, lobsters, and mussels.

Fabulous Body Fuel Fact

In the past, children were given cod-liver oil from cod fish. It tasted awful but was healthy because cod-liver oil is rich in essential fatty acids.

Protein for Vegetarians

People who do not eat meat or fish are called vegetarians. Vegetarians eat beans, nuts, and sometimes eggs for protein.

Body Fuel Health Tips

Soybeans are a little different from other beans because they have more fat. This is a polyunsaturated fat that is good for you.

Soybeans
Soybeans are high in protein and are a good source of protein for vegetarians. Soybeans are prepared in many ways all over the world. Common soybean products are soy milk, tofu, and **tempeh**.

Nuts
People have collected nuts for protein for thousands of years. There are many varieties of nuts, including cashew, macadamia, almond, pine nut, walnut, and pistachio. The most common nut is the peanut. However, the peanut is not really a nut. It is a legume, like the soybean.

Eggs
Some vegetarians eat eggs. Eggs are high in **biological protein**. People eat eggs from chickens, and sometimes from ducks and quail. Some indigenous peoples also eat eggs from wild birds and turtles.

The Digestive System

The digestive system breaks down the foods we eat so they are ready to be absorbed into the bloodstream. Each part of the digestive system plays a part in breaking down, or digesting, foods. **Saliva** and **digestive enzymes** prepare to digest foods even before we eat them. They are produced when we see or smell foods.

Mouth
Teeth cut and grind food into smaller pieces. The enzymes in saliva start to break down carbohydrates in the food. The chewed food becomes a **bolus**, which is pushed down the throat by the tongue when we swallow.

Esophagus
The bolus travels down the esophagus (ee-*soff*-a-gus) to the stomach.

Liver
The liver filters nutrients from the blood. Nutrients are sent to the small intestine for digestion. Waste is sent to the large intestine.

Stomach
Stomach muscles churn the bolus. Acid in the stomach makes the food watery.

Gallbladder
The gallbladder stores bile, which is a digestive liquid made by the liver. Bile is used in the small intestine to break down fats.

Pancreas
The pancreas makes enzymes that break down macronutrients.

Large Intestine
The large intestine is 5 feet (1.5 meters) long. It carries waste to the **rectum** for **evacuation** as **feces** (*fee-seas*).

Small Intestine
The small intestine is almost 23 feet (7 meters) long. Foods are digested in the small intestine after they are broken down in the stomach. Most nutrients are absorbed into our bloodstream through **villi** in the small intestine.

Fabulous Body Fuel Fact
A bolus takes about three seconds to reach your stomach after it is swallowed.

Fabulous Body Fuel Fact

The stomach also uses hydrochloric acid to break down proteins. Hydrochloric acid is very strong and can burn skin. And your stomach makes it!

How Does the Body Digest Meat, Fish, Eggs, Nuts, and Beans?

Special enzymes help the body digest meat, fish, eggs, nuts, and beans.

The Mouth

Digestion of protein foods begins in the mouth. Protein foods are often coarse. **Molars** help break down these foods by grinding them into a bolus.

The Stomach

The stomach makes an enzyme called pepsin to break down protein foods. Strong muscles in the stomach churn the food, just like an electric beater churns cake batter. Churning helps break the proteins into even smaller pieces.

Pancreas and Small Intestine

The pancreas sends enzymes called proteolytic (*pro*-tee-o-*lit*-ic) enzymes, such as pepsin, to the small intestine. These enzymes break down the proteins into amino acids that are absorbed into the bloodstream.

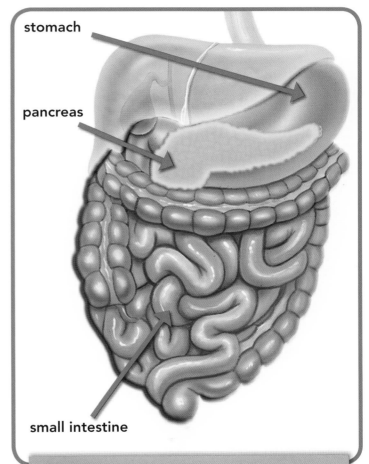

stomach

pancreas

small intestine

Proteolytic enzymes are made in the pancreas and help break down food in the small intestine.

Body Fuel Health Tips

Solid waste from the body, called feces, tells us if we are eating well. "Healthy" feces are soft and bulky. Healthy food, lots of water, and exercise ensure that the body has healthy feces.

How Does the Digestive System Absorb Meat, Fish, Eggs, Nuts, and Beans?

Proteins are absorbed into the bloodstream from the small intestine. When digested food arrives in the small intestine it is watery, like skim milk.

There are three parts to the small intestine: the duodenum, the jejunum, and the ileum. The tiny amino acids in food are absorbed from the ileum. The walls of the small intestine have little fingerlike bumps, called villi. Amino acids and other nutrients pass through the villi into the bloodstream.

Bloodstream

The bloodstream is made up of **capillaries**, **veins**, and **arteries**.

Nutrients from the villi are absorbed into the capillaries. The capillaries carry nutrient-rich blood to the arteries, which carry blood around the body.

The bloodstream carries amino acids and other nutrients to body **cells**. The nutrients even travel into the **bone marrow**, where they feed the cells with special proteins that bones need to grow.

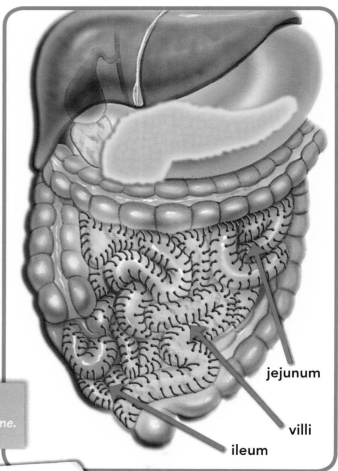

jejunum

villi

ileum

Most nutrients, including proteins, are absorbed through villi in the small intestine.

Body Fuel Health Tips

Foods such as eggs, fish, and dairy are high in biological protein. The protein in these foods comes with other healthy nutrients, giving your body a nutrient boost.

How Do Meat, Fish, Eggs, Nuts, and Beans Help the Body Function?

Protein is used in many parts of the body, such as the **organs**, muscles, bones, skin, hair, fingernails, and blood. It repairs the millions of cells in the body. Without protein foods, cells die and people get sick. Proteins can also be enzymes and antibodies.

Enzymes

Many proteins are enzymes. They perform millions of functions throughout the body, such as digesting foods.

Antibodies

Some proteins in the human body are also antibodies. These substances fight infection and disease.

Amino Acids

Proteins are made from amino acids. Humans need twenty different amino acids to build cells and body tissues. The body can make ten of these.

The other essential amino acids come from meat, fish, eggs, nuts, and beans. If people do not have all the amino acids they need, body tissue starts to break down, some hair may be lost, and fingernails may break easily.

Protein foods are needed by the cells in hair, skin, and many other parts of the body.

Body Fuel Health Tips

An essential amino acid is an amino acid that we have to get from food. This is because our body cannot make the amino acid.

What Nutrients Are in Meat, Fish, Eggs, Nuts, and Beans?

Meat, fish, eggs, nuts, and beans are full of nutrients, such as protein, vitamins, and minerals.

Nutrients in Meat, Fish, Eggs, Nuts, and Beans					
Nutrients	Red Meat	Poultry	Fish	Eggs	Nuts and Beans
Macronutrients					
carbohydrates					•
protein	•	•	•	•	•
fats and oils	•	•	•	•	•
Micronutrients					
Vitamins					
vitamin A	• (in liver)			•	
vitamin B1			•		•
vitamin B2	•	•	•		•
vitamin B3	•		•		•
vitamin B5				•	
vitamin B9				•	
vitamin B12			•	•	
vitamin D			•	•	
vitamin E					•
Minerals					
calcium					•
iron	•	•		•	•
magnesium		•			
phosphorous		•		•	•
potassium					•
zinc	•	•			•
Fatty Acids					
cholesterol	•	•		•	
marine omega-3			•		

There are many different kinds of tasty protein-rich foods.

Fabulous Body Fuel Fact

When eaten with vegetables, meat helps your body absorb the iron in vegetables.

How Does the Body Use These Nutrients?

Nutrients from meat, fish, eggs, nuts, and beans are used throughout the body. Some nutrients are stored in the liver for release when needed.

Brain
Fish is full of essential fatty acids and vitamins that fuel memory and brain enzymes.

Hair and Nails
Hair and nails are made from a protein called keratin. Keratin is made up of about twenty amino acids.

Skin
Skin is the largest organ of the body. It depends on vitamins, minerals, fat, cholesterol, and protein for cell renewal.

Internal Organs and Muscles
The heart, lungs, and muscles need protein to regrow and repair their cells. Many vitamins and minerals are also necessary for organ and muscle health.

Bones
Protein fuels cell growth in bones. The bloodstream carries nutrients to bone marrow.

Body Fuel Health Tips

People need to eat a variety of protein foods for amino acids. Eating a variety of foods gives us the essential amino acids we need for healthy bones, skin, hair, and nails.

Fueling the Body with Meat, Fish, Eggs, Nuts, and Beans

The energy in food is measured in calories or kilojoules. The amount of energy people need depends on their height, sex, and age. It also depends on the amount of exercise they do. Adolescent boys age ten to twelve doing moderate exercise need about 1,800 to 2,200 calories (7,500–9,500 kilojoules) of energy daily. Girls the same age need a bit less, about 1,800 to 2,000 cal (7,500–8,500 kJ).

You need energy to think, breathe, pump your heart, and replace protein in cells. Almost half of our energy is used to support our basal metabolic rate. This is the energy we burn just by being alive. When energy levels drop, people grow tired and the body cannot function properly.

Extra energy is stored as fat. People need to balance how much food they eat with the energy they burn during activities.

Playing and exercising burns lots of body fuel.

Body Fuel Health Tips

For healthy bodies, we need:
- beans daily
- lean meat four to five times a week
- fish twice a week
- an egg three to four times a week
- a handful of unsalted nuts three times a week.

People in developed countries often get more than one-third of their energy from animal foods. In Africa, most people get less than one-tenth of their daily energy from animal foods.

How Much Protein Energy Do I Need Each Day?

Protein has 4 cal (17 kJ) of energy per 1 gram. Young people need around 5 to 6 ounces of protein a day. This equals about 190 to 290 cal (800–1,200 kJ) from protein daily.

Some of the energy in protein foods comes from fats, such as the fat in fish and meat. Protein foods can be high in saturated fat, so choose lean meat.

Eating the right amount of protein foods helps build muscles for exercise.

Body Fuel Health Tips

Getting enough protein is easy. Cereal and milk for breakfast provide 10 g of protein. A palm-sized steak contains about 30 g of protein. One egg has 13 g of protein. Eat a cup of lentil soup after school for essential proteins. This will ensure you get the right mix of protein every day.

Healthy Food Choices

Meat, fish, eggs, nuts, and beans are healthy food choices. However, there are many different ways to prepare the protein foods we eat.

Some healthy preparation choices for protein foods are:

- steaming, which cooks foods without adding fat
- dry-roasting, which is a way of roasting food without oils or fats
- broiling, which allows fat to drain away
- boiling, which removes fats from meats

The following table shows some healthy ways to prepare and eat protein foods.

✓ Healthy Choices	✗ Less Healthy Choices
Meat	
lean meat	meat with skin and fat
broiled lean ground beef	fried, fatty meat
skinless steamed or broiled poultry	deep-fried chicken with skin
Fish	
broiled, steamed, or dry-roasted fish	battered, deep-fried fish
Eggs	
boiled eggs, poached eggs, omelettes, souffles	fried eggs, eggs with sauces
Nuts	
unsalted, dry-roasted nuts	salted nuts roasted in oils
Beans	
tempeh and tofu	deep-fried tempeh and tofu

Fabulous Body Fuel Fact

In Japan, fish is often eaten raw and is called *sushi*. This is a delicious and very healthy choice!

Lean meat that is steamed or broiled is a healthier choice than fried meat, such as fried chicken.

Fast Foods and Fresh Foods

Fast foods are often processed or cooked in fat. They may have fewer nutrients than fresh foods. Fast food is energy inefficient because it is high in fat. This means the body has to work hard to use the energy. It is only used during heavy exercise or when the body has less carbohydrate and protein energy available. Unused energy is stored as fat.

Preservatives

Highly processed fast foods often have lots of **preservatives** and chemical flavorings. They may also be high in salt and sugars. These kinds of fast foods should not be eaten more than once a week.

Body Fuel Health Tips

A fast food hamburger, large fries, and soda is a high-fat meal of about 1,200 cal (5,000 kJ). That is more than half your body's daily energy needs. The burger with no fries and a diet soda has 500 cal (2,100 kJ).

A healthier choice is a ham, cheese, and lettuce on a whole-wheat roll at just 360 cal (1,500 kJ).

A greasy hamburger has protein, but also contains lots of fat.

Functional Foods

Functional foods supply the nutrients we need daily to live. However, scientists suggest they may also have super nutrients that lower the risk of diseases. Many natural foods, such as meat, fish, nuts, eggs, and soybeans, have these super nutrients. People obtain these nutrients when they eat a fresh, healthy, balanced diet.

Discovering Functional Foods

The super nutrients in some foods were first recognized in Japan during the 1980s. Japanese health authorities believed eating health-promoting foods would help people live healthier lives. Food scientists around the world are studying these foods to understand how they work on the human body.

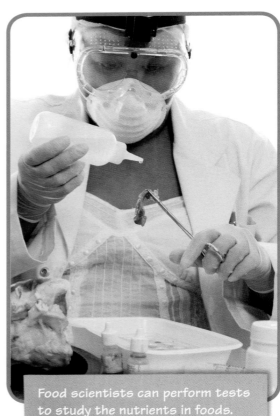

Food scientists can perform tests to study the nutrients in foods.

Fabulous Body Fuel Fact

In many parts of Asia, some people eat the gallbladder and meat of the cobra and drink its blood. They believe this can cure diabetes, cancer, and skin problems.

Cobras are poisonous snakes, but some people eat their meat for health.

Choosing Natural Functional Foods

Choosing natural functional protein-rich foods, such as fresh fish, can help you have lifelong good health. Eating functional foods with lots of fruits and vegetables and drinking six glasses of water a day may improve health and reduce some diseases.

Some functional protein foods are listed below.

Benefits of Functional Foods		
Functional Protein Food	Super Nutrients	Benefits
fish	omega-3 fatty acids	improves mental function and eyesight, reduces heart disease
soybeans	lysine	promotes healing, may reduce cold sores
eggs	folate	may reduce disease in newborn babies, needed by pregnant mothers
	lutein, zeaxanthin	promote healthy skin and eyes, may help prevent cancer
walnuts	omega-3 fatty acid	may reduce cholesterol in the blood, improves brain function

Fresh fish is a good source of omega-3 fatty acids.

Naturally Healthy Meat, Fish, Eggs, Nuts, and Beans

For thousands of years, people have grown and eaten natural foods to stay healthy. A healthy diet from across the food pyramid gives us all the nutrients we need. We also need to exercise and drink plenty of water for good health.

Balanced meals of protein-rich foods with vegetables and grains help make people naturally healthy.

Body Fuel Health Tips

To stay healthy, people can:
- eat two pieces of fruit a day
- eat five servings of vegetables a day (about 2-1/2 cups)
- eat two fish meals a week
- choose low-fat cheese, milk, and yogurt
- choose polyunsaturated and mono-unsaturated oils
- limit fast foods to once or twice a week
- always choose lean meat.

Fabulous Body Fuel Fact

Vegetarians need to eat lots of soybean foods for the essential amino acid lysine. Deficiencies in lysine can cause hair loss, stunted growth, and a lack of energy.

Staying Healthy

A natural way to stay healthy and prevent some illnesses and **deficiencies** is to:

- eat food from across the food pyramid in the right amounts
- get at least thirty minutes of exercise each day
- drink plenty of water.

Some illnesses or vitamin deficiencies may be caused by an unhealthy diet.

- Too much sugar can send **glucose** levels out of balance. This can cause diabetes.
- Too much fat can cause blockages in arteries. This can cause heart attacks.

Vitamin and mineral deficiencies can cause:

- tiredness
- poor memory
- fragile bones, which break easily.

Vitamin, Mineral, and Protein Deficiencies

Few people in developed countries get ill from vitamin, mineral, or protein deficiencies. However, due to poor diet, they may have less of these nutrients than they need. This may make people feel tired and run down.

Some people in developing countries have severe vitamin, mineral, and protein deficiencies. This can affect children's growth and even their ability to learn.

Soybeans, which provide lysine, grow inside shells called pods.

21

Meat, Fish, Eggs, Nuts, and Beans Around the World

People around the world need nutrients from meat, fish, eggs, nuts, and beans to stay healthy. People in different places eat different protein-rich foods. As you can see from this world map, people around the world eat different kinds of protein-rich foods.

Iceland, Scandinavia, and the Arctic Circle
The people in Iceland and Scandinavia eat lots of oily fish. The Inuit people of the Arctic Circle hunt fish and whale meat for much of their diet.

Arctic Circle

Iceland

United States

South America

The Netherlands
Herring is a delicacy in The Netherlands.

France
Snails and frogs are traditional specialties of France.

South America
People in South America often mix cooked beans and meat together. This is a healthy way to get important nutrients.

Fabulous Body Fuel Facts

The people of the Amazon rain forest in South America hunt wildlife, including frogs and insects, to get 85 percent of their daily protein.

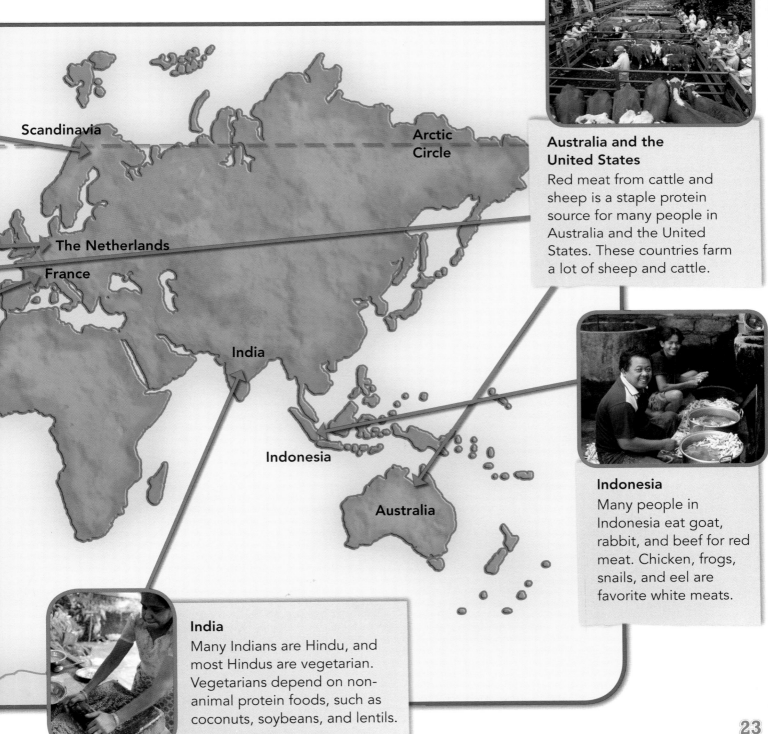

Scandinavia

Arctic Circle

The Netherlands

France

India

Indonesia

Australia

Australia and the United States
Red meat from cattle and sheep is a staple protein source for many people in Australia and the United States. These countries farm a lot of sheep and cattle.

Indonesia
Many people in Indonesia eat goat, rabbit, and beef for red meat. Chicken, frogs, snails, and eel are favorite white meats.

India
Many Indians are Hindu, and most Hindus are vegetarian. Vegetarians depend on non-animal protein foods, such as coconuts, soybeans, and lentils.

Allergies and Intolerances to Meat, Fish, Eggs, Nuts, and Beans

Food allergies and intolerances are reactions by our bodies to different foods. A food allergy occurs when the **immune system** reacts as if a food is dangerous. This reaction may cause itchy skin or make breathing difficult. A food intolerance is a negative chemical reaction in the body to the food. Food intolerances often cause similar symptoms to allergic reactions.

Common Allergies to Protein-rich Foods

Among protein foods the most common allergies or intolerances are to peanuts, nuts, eggs, seafood, and fish.

The most dangerous reaction to food is anaphylaxis in people with a severe allergy. Peanut, nut, egg, and seafood allergies are the most common cause of anaphylaxis.

Anaphylaxis

Anaphylaxis (*an*-a-fal-*ax*-is) is a severe allergic reaction. If people have this reaction they need immediate help. Anaphylaxis can happen quickly. Some of the signs of anaphylaxis are:

- trouble breathing, loud breathing, wheezing, or coughing
- the tongue or lips swelling or feeling itchy
- the throat feeling tight
- difficulty talking
- becoming unconscious
- becoming pale and limp (young children)
- an itchy rash, called hives, on the body
- a skin rash or redness, called eczema, that can get worse
- asthma
- vomiting, stomach cramps, and diarrhea.

A person who has an allergic reaction, such as asthma, may need to take medication.

What Can I Eat if I Am Allergic to Fish or Nuts?

There are many other protein-rich foods you can choose if you have a food intolerance or allergy. Fish and seafood can be replaced with lean meat, low-fat dairy, nuts, beans, and seeds. Peanuts and other nuts can be replaced with beans and seeds.

Allergy Testing

It is important to know which foods cause allergic reactions or food intolerances. Many hospitals and clinics test people for allergies so they can avoid allergy-producing foods. The most common test for allergies is called the skin-scratch test. Doctors place tiny bits of **allergens** on the skin to test for reactions. If reactions occur, the problem foods can be removed from the diet.

Lean meat can be a healthy alternative if you have an allergy to other protein-rich foods.

Body Fuel Health Tips

There is no perfect substitute for eggs if you have an allergy. However, you can choose to eat a variety of other protein foods. If you suspect you have a reaction to a food, you should ask to visit the doctor.

Checking Food Labels for Meat, Fish, Eggs, Nuts, and Beans

Many governments around the world have laws requiring packaged foods to be labeled. Food labels state how much protein, fat, sugar, and carbohydrate are in the foods. Food labels also state:

- ingredients
- use-by dates
- storage instructions (such as "keep frozen")
- additives
- flavorings.

Food labels list ingredients by weight. So, a can of baked beans made mostly from navy beans will list navy beans first and other ingredients in descending order.

Food Additives

Many packaged foods contain food additives, such as vitamins and coloring. Coloring additives are often listed by color and number such as Red #40.

Allergies

It is important for people with food allergies or intolerances to read food labels. Food labels on packaged foods usually show allergy-producing ingredients.

Body Fuel Health Tips

The most common ingredients causing food reactions are:
- shellfish
- eggs
- fish
- milk
- nuts and sesame seeds.

Nutrition Facts

Serving Size 1 egg (50g)
Servings 18

Amount Per Serving

Calories 70 Calories from Fat 40

	% Daily Value
Total Fat 4.5 g	7%
Sat. Fat 1.5 g	8%
Trans. Fat 0 g	
Cholest. 215 mg	71%
Sodium 65 mg	3%
Total Carb. Less than 1 g	0%
Protein 6 g	10%

Vitamin A 6%	•	Vitamin C 0%
Calcium 2%	•	Iron 4%

Not a significant source of Dietary Fiber or Sugars.

*Percent Daily Values are based on a 2,000 calorie diet. Your daily values may be higher or lower depending on your calorie needs.

		Calories	2,000	2,500
Total Fat	Less than	65g	80g
Sat. Fat	Less than	20g	25g
Cholesterol	Less than	300mg	300mg
Sodium	Less than	2,400mg	2,400mg
Total Carbohydrate		300g	375g
Dietary Fiber		25g	30g
Protein		50g	65g

LARGE EGG

A food label also shows how many calories the food contains.

Checking Food Labels for Healthy Eating

Food labels can help people avoid foods they may be allergic to. If you have an allergy to a protein food, you need to check for this food on labels. The following table shows foods that often contain allergy-producing protein foods.

Allergy	Foods
peanuts	cookies, breakfast cereal, chocolate, dried fruit mix, health-food bars
fish or seafood	Asian dishes, canned spreads, dips, gelatin, marshmallows, salad dressing, sauces, fish stock, seafood flavoring
soybeans	bean curd, miso, tamari, tempeh, vegetable stock, vegetable broth, flavoring (natural and artificial)
nuts	baked products, cookies, breakfast cereal, chocolate, dried fruit mix, flavoring (natural and artificial), flavored coffee, flavored drinks, health-food bars, ice cream, candy, snack foods
eggs	baked products, battered foods, cookies, cakes, candy, custards, doughnuts, frittatas, fritters, frozen desserts, glazed foods, icing, mayonnaise, hamburgers, mousse, pastries, quiche, salad dressings

It is important to check food labels carefully if you have an allergy.

Body Fuel Health Tips

Foods such as eggs can have different names on food labels. These are some of the names for egg products: albumen, apovitellin, avidin, flovoproteins, livetin, lysozyme, ovalbumin, ovglycoprotein, ovomucoid, ovomuxiod, and powdered egg.

Cooking Class

Ask an adult to help you.

Preparing healthy foods that supply nutrients from across the food pyramid is fun, easy, and delicious. Follow these recipes for Green Salad and Easy Pizza to get:

- carbohydrates for energy
- protein for cell renewal
- calcium for strong bones
- vitamin C for healthy skin
- iron for healthy blood
- fiber for healthy digestion
- minerals and B vitamins for healthy blood cells.

Green Salad

Servings   Four to six

Preparation time   15 minutes

Ingredients

6 lettuce leaves

1 cup fresh spinach leaves

1 cucumber

1 avocado

1/4 cup chopped parsley

1 tablespoon lemon juice for dressing

Preparation

1. Wash the lettuce and spinach and tear into pieces. Set aside to drain.

2. Slice the cucumber and avocado.

3. Place all ingredients in a large bowl and mix—but first, clean your hands.

lettuce leaves   avocado

spinach leaves   parsley

cucumber   lemon juice

Easy Pizza

Servings   Two to four
Preparation time   20 minutes
Cooking time   20 minutes

Ingredients

4 small pitas

4 tablespoons tomato sauce

1 cup grated cheddar cheese

1 cup chopped ham

1 large, ripe tomato, chopped

1 cup ricotta cheese

Preparation

1.   Preheat the oven to 450 degrees Fahrenheit (230 degrees Celsius).

2.   Put the pitas on a non-stick baking tray.

3.   Spoon one tablespoon of tomato sauce onto each pita. Spread the sauce over the pita with the back of the spoon.

4.   Sprinkle the cheddar cheese over the tomato sauce.

5.   Put the pitas into the oven for 7 minutes, or until the cheese is bubbling.

6.   Pull out the tray and sprinkle the ham, tomato, and ricotta over the pitas.

7.   Put pizzas into the oven for 7 to 12 minutes, or until golden.

Serve with Green Salad for a healthy, yummy meal filled with body fuel.

pitas

tomato sauce and ripe tomatoes

cheddar cheese

ham

ricotta cheese

Fueling the Body with Healthy Meat, Fish, Eggs, Nuts, and Beans

Meat, fish, eggs, nuts, and beans are the body builders of the food pyramid. These are the foods that build muscles and all the cells in the body. Weight lifters and other athletes eat lots of these foods to build their muscles. Growing children also need to eat enough protein every day.

Eating different meat, fish, eggs, nuts, and beans supplies nutrients from protein foods for good health. Two to three servings of these foods each day provide the proteins we need daily. It is that easy.

By following the healthy food pyramid and eating the right amounts of proteins, carbohydrates, and fats, people can get the right body fuel for healthy bodies.

Protein-rich foods are important to help muscles grow.

Glossary

allergens	substances in foods that cause allergic reactions
arteries	blood vessels that carry blood away from the heart
balanced diet	a mix of different foods that provides the right amount of nutrients for the body
biological protein	protein that comes from animals
bolus	a small ball of chewed food
bone marrow	a jelly-like substance inside bones
capillaries	the smallest blood vessels in the body, which allow nutrients to pass in and out of the bloodstream
cells	microscopic structures that combine to make up all the bones, muscles, and other parts of the body
chemical reactions	processes by which substances are changed into other substances
deficiencies	shortages of specific nutrients
digestive enzymes	proteins that speed up the chemical reactions involved in the digestion of food
evacuation	removal from the body
feces	solid waste that is evacuated from the body
glucose	a type of sugar
immune system	the body system that fights infections
molars	the large teeth at the back of the mouth, used for grinding foods
nutrients	substances that provide energy when eaten
organs	parts inside the body, such as the heart or lungs, that perform functions
preservatives	ingredients, such as salt, that are added to foods to make them last longer
rectum	the end of the large intestine, where feces are stored before evacuation
saliva	the fluid in the mouth that helps digest food
tempeh	a nutty-flavored food made from soybeans
veins	blood vessels that carry blood to the heart
villi	small, fingerlike bumps on the inside wall of the small intestine

Index